FOR SILVER SEE BLUE

for silver see blue

GLENN STORHAUG

BOOKS WEST FIVE HOUSE SEASONS BOOKS PRESS
PRESS FIVE WEST SEASONS HOUSE PRESS BOOKS

SHEFFIELD • HEREFORD
2003

Published in England by
West House Books, 40 Crescent Road Nether Edge, Sheffield s7 1 hn
& Five Seasons Press, 41 Green Street Hereford hri 2qh
Distributed in usa by
spd, 1341 Seventh Street, Berkeley ca 94710 - 1409

isbn 1 904052 09 6 (west house)
isbn 0 947960 15 5 (five seasons)

The photograph of the *MS Venus* on pages 16-17 is reproduced by kind permission of the Bergens Sjøfartsmuseum, Norway. (See page 24 for more about the *Venus*.) The picture of the *Elsie Beth* on page 64 reproduces a family photograph.

The photograph, on pages 8 & 52, of the *La Parisienne* fresco fragment (in the Heraklion Archaeological Museum, Crete) is reproduced by kind permission of the Ashmolean Museum, Oxford. This photograph is in the museum's Sir Arthur Evans Archive and was probably taken within a year or two of the unearthing of the fragment at Knossos (see page 62). As far as the Ashmolean's Evans Archivist knows, it has not been published before.

The painting on page 7 is the frontispiece (folio 37) to *Pearl* in the vellum manuscript (Cotton Nero A. x) of this poem—composed towards the end of the fourteenth century by an unnamed poet who was probably also the author of *Sir Gawain and the Green Knight* (also first recorded in Cotton Nero A. x). Reproduced by permission of The British Library.

More acknowledgements: page 63
Table of contents & Norwegian glossary: page 62

Designed & typeset in Jenson at Five Seasons Press, Hereford
Printed (on Five Seasons recycled paper) and bound
by MPG Books Ltd, Bodmin, Cornwall

for Finn, Anna & Max

PEARL-DIVING DISTRACTIONS
FOR STUDENTS OF MEDITATION
LOST IN AN ARBOUR

(Allas! I leste hyr in on erbere)

wake to gong

before blue-fingered dawn

walk to shell
        of unlit room
sit
        in circle —cymbal PING!—
& silence

shut eyes against
        the ocean dark
(lids lined
with oyster light)

so iridescent silvered iris
mirrors
pages of *Japon nacré*
printed
with 'impression off'

then empty
every word of breath
to read this book of blanks

until the

tail of fish dart
restless mind
flicks up clouds
from seabed sand
(where constant amber
    ma-ne
          jewel
  in *pad-me*
         lotus
              glows)

until the

irritant grain
enters the mother

Orient pearl

to glide into grass

lost & found

in the device of a dream

OXYGEN: FIRST ASCENT

face against rock face
wet smell of granite
snow grit taste of
juniper   moss
ice-scored stone
scratching skin

step back from the face
to add sky
add birch fringe below,
return to the valley—fields
fences farms

see from lowland
how it starts to be *'shān'*
'oros'   'fjell'

'mountain'

toes M
fingers O
up to U
gripped at N
piton T
pull to A
arriving I
where N (the numinous)
   don't know what's hit them
   —Aphrodite shakes
   salt water
   from her hair
      settles in
      on Mt Olympus

Italian climb is much the same
but less of a haul in Scotland
(Iceland, too, where
'fell' falls short
of 'fjall')

more rope needed
for the rock face in Finland
        (a tall story among lakes &
woods)

<pre>
                              v
                              u
                              o
                              r
                              e
        m   n
        o   s
        n   e
        t   i
        a   f   n
        g   e   ä
        n   l   m
        a   l   ä
</pre>

DEAR_SOMEBODY, UNDESIRED_LANGUAGE_BODY

'Today some Americans played Brahms in the Stavanger Konserthus. No dictionaries were needed, despite the use of a Hungarian Csárdás melody in the last movement of the G minor Quartet. No attempts were made to translate the Allegro into Faroese or Tamachek, nor were any photographs or diagrams needed to illustrate the Andante. A simultaneous translation of the Intermezzo into Greek was considered no more necessary than a glossary of the Rondo for any Chinese who might be present.'

VENUS IN TRANSIT

slow sweep against star chart

antennae impress the North Sea sky
with sympathetic strings
& underfoot
the deep persistent muffled thud
        of distant generator sheds
        muted horn's
        discovered score,
        diesel marine's
        bass rattle
piped to a different pitch
—clatter
funnelled
to whispers
        —wisp of exhaust
        against white Bear

DAY CROSSING

her bones silver
her flesh gold

sun flash
on pearl wave
curls away
from the prow

NIGHT CROSSING

stars fleck
ultramarine

tarnished
    sea's
secret
    glass
smoked
    gleam
hill
    tarn
black
    port
sky
    hole
through
    which
darkly

the Greeks
never polished
their silver

THREE GENERATOR SETS

sphere   hum   rapt   boulder

wrapped in snow & leaning starward

flicks light   earth to sky

strung   crystal   spin   sun

pick up trails of ozone scatter

shot silk   in salt speech

turquoise child

lapis sunrise

into azure

ENGINE TELEGRAPH: FULL AHEAD

when 'terminator' modifies 'generator'
winged seed
hits the ground
twisting like a tongue

when finely-turned prose
follows the plot
— but keep to the path
across the fields
where trees lean out
on spirit branches —
tongues
curl—twist—choke
DYS / DIS
-seminate & -semble

each letter salvaged
each word
hand picked
for distribution
until the case is closed

when dominant discourse surrenders
please colour the shadows
with mauves & greens,
air-vowels from sun-fire
marooned
on salt sea

brush filled with turquoise
—cerulean, viridian—
covers the canvas completely
— earth wrapped in sky —
until cymbal ping
opens eyes to dawn

pigment from lapis ultramarine
depends on diesel aquamarine
meshing the stars
in a charcoal'd cloud
but palest blue harebells still stitch
the wet meadows—
sliding past dull-red barns in the dusk,
lakes catching the last of the sky—
blue chicory by the path
blue shutters on the wall

how painted or scored
flares up pages
scanned at random
to fade again on screen

towers on tors
cliff-top pyramid beacons
point the pilot's way
— navigate instead
by sap green, grey or brown
framed by the ring of the cymbal

Marina sings Pericles out of silence,
shocks him from perpetual present
curled night and day like a cat on the deck
into memory of all the words required:
transponders hum like wind in the rigging

roll-on roll-off
raw Nordic ports he sails between
embellishing a lifetime's glosses

calling the lapsèd soul
crow call from snow-wall'd valley

calling the lapsèd soul
from stone lapp'd by snow melt

calling the lapsèd soul
where birch holds silver to blue

on the marine radio telephone
read the display screen:

VID SVAR, BETALA   (Swedish)

('feldspar be taller')

> *when feldspar inclines*
> *(at a microcline angle)*
> *towards blue and green*
> *then lapis lazuli*
> *and turquoise*
> *are night sky and joy*

('say—fable—teach')

PAY TO ENABLE SPEECH   (English)

if there's any point it probably has to do with diversity, the choice as close to infinite as makes no difference, comparing one selection with another, one scratch, stick, stave with another, forged/foreign coins jamming the appliance—otherwise cant or song of the earth cantata, every beak busy with lyric alarm

     wickers crossed
          to make the wheel
    the withies twist around

       'the common good'

thy baszkett

           willow ply on willow

Blessed shal be thy baszkett,
and thy stoare

           commons
   choked
   a tongue
         enclosed

       about speech   enable ship
       sweep, sweep of the beam

Built in Helsingör [Elsinore] 1931.

> *Up from my cabin,*
> *My sea-gown scarfed about me*

Gross tonnage 5406.

Dead weight 1700.

Speed 19.5.

Laid up in Norway September 1939.

Seized by Germans 1940.

Converted for war purposes at the Neptunwerft.

Target ship for the U-boat flotilla based at Pillau (now
    Baltiysk), outport of Immanuel Kant's Königsberg
    (now Kaliningrad).

Bombed and sunk in Hamburg harbour by allied aircraft
    March 1945.

Raised and returned to Helsingör for rebuild 1947.

Resumed North Sea crossings
        (Bergen/Stavanger – Newcastle)
                until
stripped of her ornaments for the Hotel Orion in Bergen
and broken up in Faslane, Scotland, 1968.

        once she made Eos
                (auroral immortal)
        adore mortal Orion
        now she herself adorns him

after winch whirr
tightens wet ropes around bollards
we head inland fast
on dreamy sea-legs

or wake because
the engines have stopped
rattle of davits
lowering lifeboats

each night rowing
until land disappears
each day walking
until oars might be used
      to winnow corn

heart-currency, most precious,
rates of exchange
went from bad to worse
to enable speech?

The music of the spheres! List, my Marina.

returns to rock
she turns her back
pearl through grass
shoulders glide to stone

lark over downland
    where green where fire
    where sheath of gold
    on seed head hatches
      burnet moth
                    mourning
her dark return

    quick lark quick!

her back to marble
      not yet quarried

after scrambling through hawthorn & brier

(muse for the hunted hare)

brush of
limbs on
linen the
lie of
long legs limns
lines of longing
pressed from a bed
whose forme
prints every sheet
of pillow talk
with fresh scatters
of hair, form still warm
from the scattering hare
who slept all night
with open eye

the crystal cliff
the merry mere

birch beach pebble leaf
amber chanterelle
forest floor on mountainside
far out to sea

how to lift this amber light
from salt stone,
blade's harm?
or sand drift memory
from a deep well?

how to find food
among amber leaves
returned to earth?

forever refocusing
near shifts to far
peregrine meetings
hard by the shore

laughter as leaning against the machine
keys tap into bedrock
free silicon skies
grind up bytes of stars

press paper on printer
as if to make a rubbing
of its mouth

broken circuit—give
empty socket—given

(computers remove
beards, sunglasses and hats)

feel what data are left
between finger and thumb

stylus inscribes
crocus as seen:
ideo gram
baked in the sun

honey tastes
like a new word:
mono gram
baked in the sun

a few books planted
a few trees printed

beam bounces
off chance traffic
to flicker the dial

drowned Byzantine ferry log's
scattered pages
caught in the spin

— Dame Engineer Fortuna's
roulette
       radar
              calibrations

(lest sweep of the beam
sow sterile seed
vessels in port
disable all scanners)

abled at sea
                parabolic
                    wings
        revolve
                    resolving
        incoherent
                    scatter
        to steer
                by astrology

leaning seawards
        diesel rattles
        up through deck rails
heading
        twenty-five years

    for a blue wedding

last twist of honeysuckle
from the damp June hedge
last blackbird whistle
or toss of brown curls
before the bolt slides home
on the sentence
      or member
            of a sentence
                 or period
      stop locked
          above comma
      colon cut short
jaws sprung
      period

        ~

START OF FOURTH SIGNATURE
AND STILL NOT SITTING STILL

stage   left   right
breathe   in   out
wings   flies
cramp   drop
hobble   chase
knees & back
quite seized
by unskilled sitting

1) beginning
2) middle
3) end
        means every third
        thought is my grave

(his maker's voice
        wrung
                to the curtain's last drop)

in
form
ing
this
form
this
forme
cast
in
lead
this
frame
for
a
thought
that
enters
stage
left

&
exits
stage
right
with
a
back
drop
a
grace
flow
a
wave
note
of
green

'global' preferred   [Latin *globus*]
for the name of the summit;
'earth'   [Gothic *airþa*]
      too radical ?
—no problem: the corporate
shadow still hurls
the world   [Old Norse *veröld*]
and all her train
whatever name

and 'Nature' (also known as)
may still be experienced
at several resorts:
our brochure has the details

London September 28
megaphone placards
jostle to *protest the war*
against a drawing by Picasso
clear eye and silent mouth
remembering 3,000 years

DIRECTIONS FOR THIS MORNING

for Knossos take the
road of oleander
into sunrise

for the glassy sky that later
darkens to the sea at night
take blue from Egypt

for the blue of the
feathers or folds
of the Priest-King's
crown or mantle
take a fevered dream
on moonlit stairs

but if you take the
pallor of a Priestess-Queen
for the bleached brown thighs
of a Lily Prince

then take the
blue for silver

[the painter's maroons
explode to mean signals
report about chestnuts
explain about colour
confusion of cannon
and clearly explaining
how maroons exploding
sound like cannon reporting

this report under cover
of deepest maroon
explains all about her
since what it's about
is described by abouts
meaning hither & thither
just hanging about
or about to pick chestnuts
dropped all about
and marooned
about noon]

accountable tablets
       how much honey
tall ships / stories
       scratched on clay
how much paid
       figs in the sun

tallest stories
       told by tells
storey'd strata
       heaped-up speech

dig back
       to a winter's day
when waves washed
       Odysseus
here
       here, right here
just down
       from the house
at the river mouth
       —remember
warm embers
       in heaped-up leaves
'til dawn

dream cargo
checked in the hold
—sacks of flax & saffron—
simple numbers
notched & baked
& paradise accounted

anecdotes
from the store of the mother
   goddess
of afternoon wine

air-words & earth-words
travel opposite ways
to where sea and sun conspire

photochemical pentamtummeters distilled or diluted
out-breath hexameters encrusted with salt

STORYTIME

Homer held in the air for maybe hundreds of years

until pen on papyrus could catch
each cadence of his
dancing feet
(twenty-seven thousand lines times six)

       stylus on clay
       had measured sheep and oil and cheese
       each syllable
       of harvest wheat   honey recorded & stored

       tablets torched
       —riots, corporate collapse—
       Aegean futures all foreclosed

(a dark age followed
       or call it
lyric dawn)

Phoenicians shipped the consonants
and Greeks threw in the vowels

the alphabet   a silver net
to catch each word
           sung out
     of the blue
        of the wine-black
throat of the sea

blues on silver
poets of
                    whatever century

tarnished tongue or polished
to speak true?

see red: *haematite*
try bronze

yellow: *ochre*
read gold

blue: *silicate of copper*

glint dark silver salts the air

crown of azure snow-bright stone

silver woven around each wrist

night sky lustre on goddess hair

olive silver blades the bay

'Queen's metal plating, which the moonlight forms
on the bottle-green Sea / the water bright,
but the *Green* of the water not bright'

      [alloy for teapots etc.
or did Coleridge recall,
tenth day at sea, how

                    tin

                    antimony

                    bismuth

                    lead

had softened or hardened
      every word of his printed?]

'made a different colour
      from its natural blue whiteness'

of three sons
two share the grave
dug in the war's last year
on the hill above Porthmeor beach —
a cube of cold light
dandles the six-day-old daughter
cast in lead
       & curled on the empty floor

the day's accounts
scratched on clay
sun-baked
for office use

       for memory
       the final fire

he is away again on business
the accountable man of honey
ever accountable
of figs and ships

after emplaning,
the only—
his grandson
—to smile
as he jumped

& his granddaughter
first to imagine
how a hangover
    feels
        at the wheel
            of a hearse
now great-grandson's mother
turns the birth wheel

so honey's not an ideo-
        it's a mono-
           or two syllabo-
   grams

but the three other signs?

    —just who's accountable
for the 'accountable man of honey'
familiar from the gloss he gave?

'the meaning [of these adjunct signs]
    cannot be ascertained'

but he *did* do something of the kind
dealing in charms & contracts (verbal)
for honey figs & ships

  profit &
    loss ledgers
        of clay

fine quality porridge / beer
a good bundle of reeds
wedged in memory 5,000 years
then all these tablets trashed
Baghdad April 12 / 03
Free World marines casting out Satan
save every memo at his Ministry of Oil

logos got hooked up with logic
so take any flash card you like,
utgangspunkt, ok,
and the machine says
'starting (out-go-) point'
so start with this lake
which is really the sea's
innermost reach as a fjord
whose small waves lap
to mirror sky
whose fringe of autumn maple/birch
adds lake to the palette of blue

    the -trope
of helio
        counting the steps of the sun
the turn itself
  is the angled
        flash
is the slant
  the meaning acquires

deep among mountains
read what it says
on blue water
in a black well

swatch flips
to where abbot flies
past bamboo brush
points of beech
branches the breeze
knits to funnel
¡laughter!
in a scatter of ink
—hilarity of honey
heather gold
by terracotta-bellied teapot—

into the iris sky of her eyes at dawn

[INTERMITTENT FAULT]

while crooks, impostors, Taoist twisters
abduct the abbot on the purloined scroll

— hop-scotch'd serpentine meanings
push frame by frame
back through lore as recalled
through lights of the abbey
where green of the oak-hill
gleams on to grass on the floor of the nave

(reds through maroon to blue
    hummed
        radio
            from granite,
                rock   canvas   yellows
                    more rapeseed than amber)

            unaccountably

            countless &

            every

            one

            accountable

            of figs and ships

[INTERMITTENT INSULT DRUM SONG]

(accountable Chief of Beijing
Secret Police
looted temples and laundered the lot
back home in Norway
then eighty years later
New Ageing gangsters from England
raided the cloisters that blue-brushed dawn
to fence the scrolls for a corporation
— good as whose word
when flower-of-makers Chaucer's worth a turd?)

offer
song
in first bronze
light

listing star
board the blue
the wide
eyed
offing

theological rating:
'satellite goddess'

(*vid svar betala*)

List, my Marina

DIESEL RECAP

when cymbal ring sings
   end
of endless night

    city's hum
grows as rose
   finger
     paints
       high curtain walls

   thrum
of
   work-
song
    diesels
down
   below
keeping
    time
as sun
    climbs
      sea road

KNOSSOS, CHAUCER AND YOU

your yën to wol sle me sodenly
I may the beauté of hem nat sustene

. . . words unearthed . . .
how they *stongen were*
unto the herte when they
saw her first
after 3,000 years (à peu près)

sin I am free, I counte [Love] not a bene

your eyen two still slay me sodenly
I still count love a bene

O

Parisienne

minoenne !

in frame-story stone-blue windows
    a swathe-swatch of green
        lanced by lights of the abbey

burnt sienna
    on broad brush
for abstracts of
    elegies
love poems
    haiku
company profiles

sonnet suite suit sonata
observing the rubric
    the orders of service
safe from the shades
gathered in groves
    hungry for madder, cadmium,
        cuprous oxide,

        blood

Dear ————

*   I'll have to be brief*
as this winter
I'm having
no end of visits
from objective correlatives
of one sort or another:
some immediate family
and others distant cousins
not seen for thirty years.
They've all made themselves
at home: some play music
late into the night while others
are painting my kitchen
in colours of their choice.

*   This postcard shows a collage*
of all the recognition and reunion scenes
in Shakespeare.

sunray alchemic vessel
floats an inch of amber on a blue flame
where the glare of rapeseed
pressed into oil
boils out bubbles
breathed by the Baltic
and trapped in the Oligocene

clouded Inuit beads
in a muffled drum song
turned to catch occasional light
from wave wash tipped
by tide by sun

poems sung into air below zero
       into heat shimmer
where lizards dart

confusing profit & loss
they cross the lines
of double-entry columns
where linear characters
do business

keeping meaningful tally
on tablets of clay
scribes do not sing

sunset irrigation of tomato pepper aubergine
'purple and slow under their broad leaves'
'a species of fruit called melinzane'
malum insanum /mad-love-apple;
standing by the history of a word,
apophthegm, say
— white-&-blue flagged
under Greek sky
or bound around
the first *Ulysses* printing,
burnt fragrant *rigani*
—joy of the mountain—
refuge again
for a scoundrel?

       (Egyptian joy was turquoise)

position each angled face
this way and that
to catch, refract a fraction
of what's going on
—hearts and tongues—
(goats & monkeys!)

each novel page
showing its age

follow the plot
with tires screeching
guns blazing
into *that* dark wood
pricks of purposeful fire
bright red hunting jackets
converging
on nothing

skewed grey shutters bang in the wind
open and close
on the ravings of owls

hold on to the story
in outcrops of limestone
seen here & there
like a rolling whale-back
under waves of scrub
of holm oak
of lost plots
of oak ache

form found
        (her first breath)
rolls back
        to rough stone

granite for birch
        sandstone
for hawthorn & brier

as eyes return
                to iris sky
as harebells heal
        the way she went

meadow enclosed
        pearl gone to grass
& lost for words

full points removed,
seed commas curling
broad net cast

to sew that blue across canvas
at the first
        flood-lit
        glace
        of morn

ideo
hexa
hiero
calli
crypto
logo
picto
scatter
helio

     gram

by action of
turquoise
sunlight
on water

as cymbal
    PING!

opens eyes to dawn

THANKS AND ANOTHER ACKNOWLEDGEMENT

First and foremost my gratitude to you, Donna, μοῦσα beyond this poem. And many thanks to friends who gave encouragement and criticism: Alan Halsey at West House Books, Paul Merchant, John Waterfield and Nick Wong. And thanks too to the scholars who generously answered my questions about Ancient Egyptian colours, Minoan wall paintings and Tibetan symbols: Professor John Baines, Dr Katja Goebs and Dr Susan Sherratt in Oxford and Gordon Cranmer at Utstein Kloster in Norway (who also provided weathertight shelter from the storm when North Sea crossings were resumed). Special thanks to Crispin Thornton-Jones for the two paintings reproduced on the cover; thanks also to Julian Barnard. *Mange takk også* to Sverre & Kirsten Meyer-Knutsen in Kvinesdal, and to Ragnar & Laureen Meyer-Knutsen in another *dal*, Locust Valley NY, for support.

The digitalized Linear B script on pages 45 and 46 is courtesy of Curtis Clark, Biological Sciences, California State Polytechnic University, Pomona, CA 91768.

berth

On the funnel LS for father: **L** expansive, **_S_** condensed
bold italic leaning into the next business

On the bow **ELSIE BETH** for mother: evenly measured
sans-serif on a trim hull with laden hold

birth

(registered 1947)